AWESOME ACHIEVERS IN SCIENCE

AWESOME ACHIEVERS IN SCIENCE

BY ALAN KATZ

ILLUSTRATIONS BY CHRIS JUDGE

RP|KIDS
PHILADELPHIA

To all of the teachers in my life; they're true Awesome Achievers.

Running Press Kids
Hachette Book Group
1290 Avenue of the Americas, New York, NY 10104
www.runningpress.com/rpkids
@RP_Kids

Printed in the United States of America

First Edition: August 2019

Published by Running Press Kids, an imprint of Perseus Books, LLC, a subsidiary of Hachette Book Group, Inc. The Running Press Kids name and logo is a trademark of the Hachette Book Group.

The Hachette Speakers Bureau provides a wide range of authors for speaking events. To find out more, go to www.hachettespeakersbureau.com or call (866) 376-6591.

The publisher is not responsible for websites (or their content) that are not owned by the publisher.

Print book cover and interior design by Christopher Eads.

Library of Congress Control Number: 2018951804

ISBNs: 978-0-7624-6338-1 (paperback), 978-0-7624-6337-4 (ebook)

LSC-C

10 9 8 7 6 5 4 3 2 1

TABLE OF CONTENTS

~~~~~~~~~~~~~~~~~~~~~~~~~~~~~~~~~~

A Note from Alan Katz.................................. VI

Meet Michael Collins................................. 1

Meet Dr. Henry Heimlich............................. 9

Meet Dr. Patricia Bath 17

Meet George de Mestral........................... 23

Meet Dr. James Jude 31

Meet Katharine Blodgett...........................37

Meet Edwin Land 45

Meet Stephanie Kwolek 53

Meet Dr. Sally Ride................................. 61

Meet Dr. Roy J. Plunkett...........................67

Meet Dr. Spencer Silver and Arthur Fry 73

Meet Dr. Hugh Herr................................ 79

A Final Word from Alan Katz.........................86

A NOTE FROM ALAN KATZ

What's an Awesome Achiever? It's someone who's Awesome. And an Achiever.

In this book, you'll find out about twelve such people. They're scientists who've shared their genius-osity (not a word, but you know what I mean) with the world.

Their inventions and discoveries have made us healthier, smarter, happier, and safer. It's likely that you'll be familiar with their work, and yet, it's also likely that you've never heard of most of these folks.

As I tell you about these Awesome Achievers in science, I'll also be giving you my own insights into their lives and careers.

Am *I* Awesome? Am I an Achiever? Not exactly. But Mrs. Anna Bailowitz, my third-grade teacher, once said I was a nice boy.

That was good enough for me. And it made my parents happy.

I hope this book makes *you* happy.

I'll get out of the way now—so you can find out about some Awesome Achievers in science.

Enjoy . . . and thanks!

—ALAN

MEET MICHAEL COLLINS

I magine taking a road trip across the country to the greatest theme park in the world . . . and then not even getting out of the car. That's kind of what Michael Collins did as he soared to the moon but didn't get the chance to step onto it.

Michael Collins has a storied history in the U.S. Military and NASA (National Aeronautics and Space Administration) programs. He began his career as a graduate of the United States Military Academy (go Army!) and entered the United States Air Force in the early 1950s. While in the Air Force, he became a major general; he flew F-86 Sabre fighters in France and then visited air force bases in other countries as an instructor on the maintenance and flying of new aircraft. That experience allowed him to accumulate the necessary number of flight hours required to apply for the United States Air Force Experimental Test Pilot School; in 1960, his classmates included future astronauts Frank Borman (Apollo 8, Gemini 7 missions) and Jim Irwin (Apollo 15).

His decision to join NASA—a relatively new program at the time—came after watching John Glenn's 1962 Mercury-Atlas 6 flight. The idea of orbiting the Earth in just ninety minutes dazzled him (who *wouldn't* feel that way?) and he simply had to apply. Major General Collins was accepted in 1963, and after he completed a demanding training program, he was assigned to Gemini 10. Gemini 10's three-day mission was to rendezvous with another spacecraft in orbit (astronaut Collins was the first to spacewalk from one spacecraft to another) and perform medical, technical, and scientific experiments.

After that, astronaut Collins was assigned to Apollo 11, the first manned flight to the moon. Given that he was the only crewmember with spaceflight experience, he was selected as command module pilot—which meant he was to remain on board the Columbia while Neil Armstrong and Buzz Aldrin famously walked the surface of the moon. Now, you might think astronaut Collins was lonely while flying solo approximately 250,000 miles from home. It's only natural to think that. *I'd* certainly be lonely up there. Scared, even. I'd probably also feel a little left out. But none of that was true for astronaut Collins.

Although it has been said that "not since Adam has any human known such solitude," astronaut Collins knew that he was quite important to the mission. In his autobiography, he wrote that "this venture has been structured for three men, and I consider my third to be as necessary as either of the other two." During the forty-eight minutes of each orbit that he was out of radio contact with Earth, the feeling he reported was not loneliness but rather "awareness, anticipation, satisfaction, confidence, almost exultation (joy)."

Astronaut Collins was a vital part of the successful Apollo 11 mission; without him, Neil Armstrong and Buzz Aldrin would not have been able to walk the surface of the moon. And though he never personally touched the planet, astronaut Michael Collins did touch our lives by being one of only twenty-four humans to fly to the moon.

Astronaut Michael Collins also designed the famous patch that the Apollo 11 pilots wore.

Here's what it would have looked like if I had drawn it:

I ONCE ORBITED PLUTO ALL BY MYSELF! I WALKED COMPLETELY AROUND HIM AT DISNEYLAND!

IN TERMS OF APPROXIMATE SIZE, IF THE EARTH WERE A BASKETBALL, THE MOON WOULD BE A TENNIS BALL (BUT A LOT LESS FUZZY).

I WONDER IF NEIL ARMSTRONG COMPLAINED ABOUT HAVING MOON ROCKS IN HIS SHOE? I HATE WHEN THAT HAPPENS!

THE MOON'S DIAMETER IS ONE-FOURTH THE SIZE OF THE EARTH'S. MAYBE THEY TOLD MICHAEL COLLINS IT WAS TOO SMALL FOR THREE PEOPLE TO WALK ON!

ASTRONAUT COLLINS WAS BORN ON HALLOWEEN. MAN, IS A SPACE SUIT A COOL COSTUME!

A POEM CALLED ORBITING

(Not written by astronaut Michael Collins, but based on his experiences)

It's quite tranquil here in space.
You cannot see another face.
Orbiting, I must be cautious.
I got chills. I'm kinda nauseous.
My crewmates said, "We'll see ya later."
They're out playing in a crater.
Just circling, I sit, I stare.
No gravity, no solitaire.
I'll pick up Neil and Buzz real soon.
And ask, "So guys, how was the moon?"
I'll tell 'em it is good to see 'em.
And wonder what it's like to be 'em.

MEET DR. HENRY HEIMLICH

• • • • • • • • • • •

Subdiaphragmatic. It sounds like a word that Mary Poppins might sing about. But it's not. It's the first word in the term *subdiaphragmatic pressure,* which was the original name of what is now commonly known as the Heimlich maneuver.

Henry Heimlich was a New York–trained thoracic surgeon (a surgeon who's specially trained to operate on organs in the chest, generally the lungs and the heart). He was a man of true innovation throughout his entire career. During the Vietnam War, Dr. Heimlich created a chest valve drain—a tube that was inserted through bullet wounds to prevent lungs from collapsing. His invention was credited with saving many lives. "I'll admit that a number of my ideas are controversial and unorthodox," he once said. "But I have enough guts to know that when I am right, it will come about as the thing to do."

In 1972, while director of surgery at Jewish Hospital in Cincinnati, Dr. Heimlich read an article about the thousands of accidental deaths from choking that occurred every year. At that time, when a piece of food lodged in someone's throat, the widely recommended methods were to repeatedly slap that person on the back or put your fingers in his throat.

But those approaches were often ineffective; in fact, they sometimes sent the object deeper into the throat, causing—rather than preventing—death by suffocation. So, from 1972 to 74, Dr. Heimlich led a team of researchers in an effort to find a better way to save choking victims. They experimented on each other—and on dogs—until they came up with an answer.

The result was what Dr. Heimlich called subdiaphragmatic pressure—the process of getting behind the person who's choking, placing a fist below the rib cage and above the navel, and pushing in and exerting pressure upward. That movement creates a flow of air that can force objects out of the windpipe, thus allowing the choking victim to breathe freely.

Word soon spread about the doctor's discovery.

And not long after it was introduced, editors from the *Journal of the American Medical Association* called Dr. Heimlich to say they wanted to change the name from subdiaphragmatic pressure to a term that included his name. They asked if he wanted to call it the Heimlich Method or the Heimlich maneuver, informing him that a maneuver was something that involved an expert movement, while a method described something that involved a series of steps. Noting its simplicity, Dr. Heimlich immediately shouted, "Call it a maneuver!"

And that's how the Heimlich maneuver was born.

The Heimlich maneuver is indeed simple to do; it's reported that a six-year-old saved a five-year-old's life with it, and at age ninety-six, Dr. Heimlich himself saved an eighty-seven-year-old woman by using his maneuver. It's effective—estimates say that it's responsible for saving more than fifty thousand lives. And it's what makes Dr. Henry Heimlich an Awesome Achiever in science.

I'M THE M-A-N IN MANEUVER!

Many, many scientists give the world something important yet never become household names. How did Dr. Heimlich become so well-known? For one thing, unlike many scientific discoveries, his maneuver touched millions of lives because it was something most anyone could do. And also . . . his second cousin was an actor who was very popular in 1974: Anson Williams, who played the character Potsie on the sitcom *Happy Days*. (The actor's real name was Anson William Heimlich.)

When Anson Williams appeared on talk shows, he had the shows book Dr. Heimlich (whom he considered an uncle) to demonstrate his life-saving maneuver.

Man, I wish *my* second cousin would book me on a talk show. What would I demonstrate? What else but . . . the Katz maneuver.

What's the Katz maneuver, you ask?

It's another way of saying Epishouldertappitytap Pressure.

What's Epishouldertappitytap Pressure, you ask?

It's my maneuver for tapping someone on the shoulder to get his or her attention.

It's foolproof. And I'm just the fool to prove it.

I'd ask my second cousin to book me on a talk show, and he's standing just across the room, but . . . his back is turned to me and I simply can't get his attention.

THE KATZ MANEUVER

AN ODE TO DR. HEIMLICH

(to the tune of "Yankee Doodle")
Chew your food well all the time.
When eating, don't be joking,
or you'll cough, and you may find
you're absolutely choking!
Just push upward with a fist.
Follow Dr. Heimlich.
His maneuver's proved to be
a works-most-every-time trick!

Okay, okay, I know that "Heimlich" and "works-most-every-time trick" don't rhyme that well. I'm sorry. I wish the inventor of this maneuver was Dr. Reething. Then I could have ended the song . . .
Just push upward with a fist.
Follow Dr. Reething.
His maneuver's sure to help
folks regain normal breathing.

Still don't like it? Well then, I wish the inventor's name was Dr. Ruction. Then we'd be able to sing . . .
Just push upward with a fist.
Follow Dr. Ruction.
His maneuver's a great way
to dislodge an obstruction.

No, huh? In that case I have one more, *brilliant* idea. *YOU WRITE A SONG!*

* * * * * * * * * *

Speaking of talk shows, in 1978, I was working on a talk-variety show called *Kids Are People Too*. One episode featured Shelley Bruce (who was playing the title character in the Broadway musical *Annie*) and Dr. Henry Heimlich. I remember him being a very, very nice man.

The kids in the audience that day are now about fifty years old. And I can't help but wonder two things:

1. Did they ever save a life with the skills they learned from Dr. Heimlich that day?

2. Have they ever really gotten the song "Tomorrow" out of their heads?

* * * * * * * * * *

MEET
DR. PATRICIA BATH

. . . .

Sight, hearing, smell, taste, touch. A recent online survey posed the question: if you had to give up one of your senses, which would you choose? Not surprisingly, only 1.8 percent said they would go without sight, thereby declaring it the most precious of all senses.

It's so very important not to take vision for granted; checkups can help keep your eyes healthy and strong. But when an older relative might face blindness due to a condition known as cataracts (formations that make vision cloudy), they likely can have them removed thanks to our next Awesome Achiever, Dr. Patricia Bath.

A true medical pioneer and the first African American

to complete a residency in ophthalmology (specializing in eye and vision care), Dr. Bath is responsible for saving the eyesight of thousands of people. How? you might ask. By inventing a device—the Laserphaco Probe—that can remove cataracts and often prevent blindness.

Dr. Bath's career is truly one of "firsts." In 1975, Dr. Bath became the first female faculty member in the Department of Ophthalmology at UCLA's Jules Stein Eye Institute. One year later, she cofounded the American Institute for the Prevention of Blindness, which was established on the principle that "eyesight is a basic human right." In 1983, Dr. Bath was appointed chair of the ophthalmology residency program at Drew/UCLA, again becoming the first woman in U.S. history to hold such a position.

Imagine developing a way to improve—and even restore—a person's sight. Well, Dr. Bath did more than imagine it. . . . she discovered it! In 1988, after more than five years of research and testing, Dr. Bath became the first African American female doctor to receive a medical patent—for her invention of the Laserphaco Probe. The Laserphaco Probe uses lasers to offer patients a less painful and more precise treatment of cataracts. It can also be used to return sight back to those who have suffered from blindness. "The ability to restore sight is the ultimate reward," Dr. Bath said, after doing just that for a woman in North Africa who'd been blind for thirty years.

In 2000, Dr. Bath's research took her far beyond lasers, as she received a patent to use ultrasound technology to treat cataracts.

Dr. Bath has dedicated her life and career to the prevention, treatment, and cure of blindness. Today, she is also deeply involved in telemedicine, aiming to provide medical services for those in remote areas through the use of telecommunication (transmission of voice, text, and data via electronic devices).

How many people have been saved from blindness because of the work of Dr. Patricia Bath? Perhaps hundreds of thousands. Maybe even millions. It's hard to say. But one thing is certain: if you lined them all up, they would stretch as far as the eye can see.

A SHORT (BUT TERRIFIC) POEM ABOUT VISION

You can cross the street.
You can cross your t's.
You can cross a bridge.
Cross your legs, if you please.
You can cross a river.
You can cross your heart.
But don't cross your eyes—
'cause that's not too smart.

I "SENSE" THIS IS AN IMPORTANT THOUGHT

Dr. Bath and other researchers help improve how people see.

Audiologists help improve how people hear.

Ear, nose, and throat doctors help improve how people taste.

Neuroscientists help improve people's sense of touch.

Perfume makers help improve how people smell.

FROM THE MESSY DESK OF ALAN KATZ

I'll admit it: I would have made a terrible doctor. Oh, sure, I like science. I even like research. But unlike Dr. Bath, who has had a laser-like focus on helping people (Ha! She used lasers and I said her focus was laser-like. Good joke, right?), I'm not that interested in improving anyone's life.

Oh, sure, if my kids get cuts while doing something they probably shouldn't be doing, I'll grab a bandage and toss it to them. If they get poison ivy, I'll put some lotion in their room (and then run before they come near me). And if they have a runny nose, I'll generously throw them a box of tissues.

I'm a great dad, aren't I?

But I think I'd be annoyed if my job involved fixing people's complaints. If I were a doctor, I'd say things like, "You've got a headache? Quit bellyaching. Or rather, headaching. Go home and take a nap before you give me a headache, too." Or, "Your ear is ringing? Don't answer it."

My mother had a famous saying. I'm not sure she invented it, but she said it every time I went to play football or wanted to do anything that she considered dangerous. It was, "If you break your leg, don't come running to me!"

That's the kind of medical advice I'd give. So do yourself a favor: next time you don't feel well, absolutely, positively don't call me.

MEET GEORGE DE MESTRAL

• • • • • • • • •

Some Awesome Achievers save eyesight. Others save lives. And others, well, save kids' clothes from falling off.

George de Mestral is such a man.

Born in Switzerland, Mr. de Mestral spent his lifetime as an inventor. In fact, he got his first patent—for a toy airplane—at the age of twelve (the patent protected his rights as the inventor of the toy plane). A person who craved learning and loved science, he got a degree in engineering at the École polytechnique fédérale de Lausanne.

Mr. de Mestral spent his early career as an engineer.

Then in 1948, when this curious outdoorsman was walking in the woods with his dog, he brushed against a burdock plant and realized that the burrs (spiny seed pods) were clinging to his clothes. They were even attaching themselves to his pup's fur.

Mr. de Mestral brought some of the burrs home and examined them under a microscope. What he saw inspired him: thousands of tiny hooks that held on to virtually any fabric, animal fur, or human hair.

Mr. de Mestral then set about to create a man-made form of the burrs that would serve to fasten things when combined with just the right loops of fabric. A hook-and-loop fastener was a brilliant idea. But as with many brilliant ideas, it was difficult to execute.

Many manufacturers tried and failed to create the right fibers. And it wasn't until 1955 that Mr. de Mestral applied for—and received—a patent for his invention. He named the product, and his company, Velcro®, which smashed together the beginnings of the French words *velours* (velvet) and *crochet* (hook).

When Velcro was first introduced as a "zipperless zipper," people didn't really seem to care about it. But NASA (the National Aeronautics and Space Administration) sure did; they used it to keep astronauts' gear from floating around in rockets. Velcro got a lot of attention due to its role in space missions, and soon designers started using it as a space-age fabric. Suddenly, it became a popular item and a commercial success.

Today, Velcro is used on kids' clothing, sports gear, footwear, and so much more. Think about all the things it holds together in your life, such as the backpack you probably left in school so that you can't do tonight's homework. But don't worry; what's inside the backpack is safe, 'cause it's closed tight with Velcro.

Velcro. A fasten-ating discovery, don't you think?

AN EXCLUSIVE INTERVIEW WITH MR. DE MESTRAL'S DOG

ALAN: Were you there when Mr. de Mestral found the burdock plant that led to the discovery of Velcro?

DOG: *Bark. Grrrr. Woof. Howl.*

ALAN: Would you please speak English?

DOG: Oh, sorry. Was I *there*? Yes! *I* was the one who jumped into the plant and got those pesky burrs all over me. I pulled Old Georgie over to the plant so that he could experience the same thing.

ALAN: What did Old Georgie . . . I mean, Mr. de Mestral, say?

DOG: His exact words were, "Bad dog, bad dog! Hey . . . this stuff is so clingy, it could make a great fastener."

ALAN: Is that true?

DOG: No, but it sounds good, right?

ALAN: Are you really the dog that was with Mr. de Mestral that day?

DOG: No, I'm sorry, I'm not.

ALAN: Would you please leave?

DOG: Wait . . . would you believe I was there the day Dr. Henry Heimlich invented the . . .

ALAN: No. Are you leaving?

DOG: Not until you pay me $1 millon.

ALAN: I'm not paying you $1 million.

DOG: How about $50,000?

ALAN: No.

DOG: $1.17?

ALAN: No.

DOG: Can I have a cookie?

ALAN: No. Please leave.

DOG: I can't.

ALAN: Why not?

DOG: We're stuck together with Velcro. Say, did I ever tell you about the time I took Old Georgie de Mestral to the burdock plant that led to the discovery of Vel . . .

ALAN: Sigh.

RAISE YOUR I.Q. 9,000 POINTS INSTANTLY

You might already know this, but since I don't really know you, I don't know exactly what you know, ya know?

What I want to tell you is that the "®"symbol after the word Velcro tells the world that the company has officially trademarked the product with the United States Patent and Trademark Office. By doing that, no other company can use its name (the "®" symbol is pronounced "Circle R"). Anytime you see the word in print, it has to carry that "®". Fortunately, you don't have to *say* "Circle R" each time you talk about it. Can you imagine?

A parent would say, "Jimmy, come here and let me Velcro Circle R your shoes. Then I'll Velcro Circle R your gloves. After that, I'll Velcro Circle R your pants and jacket."

*If you see a "™" symbol on a product, it means a company wants to protect its product's name (or logo's or slogan's) rights but has not officially registered it with the U.S. Patent and Trademark Office.

JUST WONDERING...

People say, "Button your lip."
They also say, "Zip your lip."
But I've never heard anyone say, "Velcro® your lip."
I don't know why I think of these things. I just do.

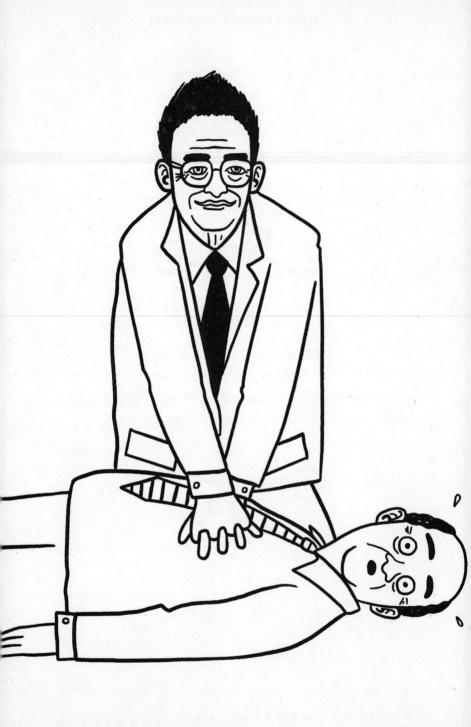

MEET
DR. JAMES JUDE

• • • • • • • • • • •

When movies promise "heart-stopping excitement," that's a good thing. It means that the film is full of thrills, and the chances are excellent that your heart won't actually stop.

But when a person's heart *does* stop, it's time to leap into action to help them survive. And that very often involves the use of cardiopulmonary resuscitation—better known as CPR.

CPR is a technique that helps save lives during heart attacks, near-drownings, and other emergency situations; it was developed by Dr. James Jude about sixty years ago. Until Dr. Jude introduced the technique, if a person's heart stopped, doctors were forced to cut open his or her chest to perform heart massage by hand to try to get it beating once again. Here's how Dr. Jude helped change all of that:

In the late 1950s, Dr. Jude was a resident (graduate student) at the Johns Hopkins University School of Medicine in Baltimore, Maryland. Two medical researchers were working in the same facility, perfecting the defibrillator—a now-much-used device that sends electric shocks to the heart in case of cardiac arrest. (You often see defibrillators on the walls of office buildings and even on some airplanes.)

The engineers, testing the early defibrillator on dogs, realized that when it was pressed against a dog's chest, the weight of its paddles encouraged cardiac activity.

Observing their work, Dr. Jude suggested that when a defibrillator wasn't available, it was possible that similar regular, rhythmic pressure could be applied to the center of the chest with the heel of the hand—to raise a person's blood pressure and help maintain circulation and breathing until medical help was available.

Dr. Jude and his collaborators first called their breakthrough "heart-lung resuscitation." Dr. Jude's wife challenged him to perform the procedure one hundred times before sharing it with the world, which he did—to great success. Not long after, in 1963, the American Heart Association endorsed the approach, changing its name to "cardiopulmonary resuscitation" (they thought that sounded more professional).

A professional-sounding name, yes. But Dr. Jude's technique does not have to be performed by a professional doctor. Indeed, lifeguards and ordinary people can easily learn CPR and continue Dr. Jude's legacy of saving lives. The use of CPR can even double or triple a heart attack victim's chance of survival.

The *Journal of the American Medical Association* compared the development of CPR to that of penicillin (one of the most widely used antibiotic medicines). But the truly humble Dr. Jude once said this about his breakthrough: "It was just . . . being in the right place at the right time and working on something for which there was an obvious need. Things like that happen in medicine all the time."

I know you join me in giving thanks to Dr. Jude and all the researchers who've saved so many lives. What kind of thanks? *Heartfelt* thanks.

A MUSICAL APPRECIATION OF DR. JUDE

(to the tune of "Hey Jude")

Hey, Dr. Jude,

you did great work.

Saving people with your pro-ce-ee-dure.

Heart patients consider you quite a star,

'cause your CPR

can make things better!

IMPORTANT MATH! IMPORTANT MATH! IMPORTANT MATH!

Your heart beats about 69 times a minute. That's about 4,140 times an hour, or 100,000 times a day. At that rate, it'll beat approximately 35 million times in a year . . . and more than 2.5 billion times over the course of your life. Be good to your heart, 'cause it's sure working hard for you.

KEEPING YOUR BODY IN "TUNE"

In 2012, the American Heart Association did a campaign urging people to learn CPR—by practicing the technique to the tune of the Bee Gees' disco hit, "Stayin' Alive."

Was it because of the catchy tune's title? Perhaps. But there was an even bigger reason—the song's tempo has 103 beats per minute, and that's just about the same rate as the number of chest compressions per minute recommended when performing CPR.

"Just push hard and fast and sing Stayin' Alive, said Dr. Alson Inaba, the pediatrician and University of Hawaii professor who matched the song with the technique.

Pretty cool. I never would have thought of that. In fact, I'd probably have come up with something like Elton John and Kiki Dee's "Don't Go Breaking My Heart"—which wouldn't have been a good choice at all.

MEET KATHARINE BLODGETT

. . . .

Here's an Awesome Achiever that achieved her awesomeness nearly a century ago. As a girl in the early 1900s, Katharine Blodgett displayed a unique mastery of mathematics and physics. And after attaining a master's degree at the University of Chicago, she became the first female to earn a PhD in physics from Cambridge University in England.

After that, she returned to the United States and moved back to her hometown of Schenectady, New York, where she joined General Electric as a research scientist— again, a "first" for a woman. While at GE, she developed thin coatings—comprising forty-four layers of liquid soap—that allowed her to create nonreflective glass that appeared invisible yet still allowed 99 percent of light to pass through without distortion. This discovery was used on eyeglasses to reduce eyestrain (it still is!), and on film camera lenses and movie projectors, among other things. Today, such anti-reflective glass can be seen (and looked through!) on windshields, telescopes, store windows, picture frames, and display showcases. It's even used on glass for picture frames so that you can clearly see the picture behind the glass. In a sense, what Ms. Blodgett pioneered was a way to make glass invisible; she's perhaps the first inventor to devise something that people *can't see*!

What's more, Ms. Blodgett invented a "glass" ruler, which measures molecular coatings on glass, down to one millionth of an inch. (*Molecular* means involving molecules; molecules are the smallest unit of a chemical compound that can take part in a chemical reaction.)

During World War II, Ms. Blodgett's coatings aided in the deicing of airplane wings. She was also instrumental in the development of improved smoke screens and gas masks, which saved soldiers' lives by protecting them from exposure to toxic smoke.

In all, Ms. Blodgett spent five decades—her entire career—at General Electric. Over that time (while holding or co-holding eight patents for humidity detectors and other devices), she was the recipient of numerous awards, including the Photographic Society of America Progress Medal and the Annual Achievement Award from the American Association of University Women. What's more, the Institute of Physicals named their business and innovation medal to honor her contributions to physics in industry; it's called the Katharine Burr Blodgett Medal and Prize to recognize her contributions to physics in industry.

Widely regarded as an outstanding researcher and chemist, Ms. Blodgett was responsible for discoveries that dramatically improved lives, both at war and at home. And by the way, if you're reading this book through eyeglasses, Ms. Blodgett is the reason you're able to see the pages without eyestrain or glare from lamps or overhead bulbs. Wow, was she a *vision*ary!

CHECK YOUR VISION (SORT OF!)

Whether or not you wear eyeglasses, you can use this handy-dandy eye chart to see how well you see, see?

I

A M

S O G L

A D Y O U A

R E R E A D I

N G T H I S B O

O K T H A N K Y O U

FACT! FACT! FACT! FACT! (MAYBE!)

I recently read that 64 percent of all American people wear eyeglasses, and 11 percent wear contact lenses.

I *think* that's what the article said. Frankly, I didn't have my eyeglasses on at the time, so it *might have* said that 34 percent of all American people like swiss cheese, and 44 percent contact their cousins every day. Or, it might've said that 43 percent of all Swiss people like american cheese, and 66 percent dunk their doughnuts in spaghetti sauce.

I apologize for not being clearer about this information, and I was afraid not wearing my eyeglasses when I read the article would reflect badly on me. But thanks to Ms. Blodgett, my eyeglasses don't reflect at all!

⋛ GENIUS! (ALMOST!) ⋛

So, I was driving my car, and my twin sons were in the back seat. It was getting dark, and I put my (anti-reflective) eyeglasses on so that I could see better. One of my sons said, "Hey, Dad, I just had a brilliant idea!"

I said, "What's that, David?"

He said, "Prescription windshields! Instead of wearing those eyeglasses to drive at night, you could just have a windshield with glass made out of the prescription you need. Incredible, right?"

I said, "Um, I'm glad you're thinking, and your idea is great in theory. But I'm afraid it has a few problems you'd need to overcome."

"Like what?" David asked.

"Well, for one thing," I said. "since I only wear these eyeglasses at night, I'd need a different windshield for daytime, wouldn't I?"

"Oh, yeah," David said.

"Besides," I added. "If your mom drives my car, she wouldn't be able to see out of the window if the windshield were customized to *my* prescription."

"Oh, yeah," David said sadly.

"*I* just had two brilliant ideas," David's twin, Nathan, said.

"What'cha got, Nathan?" I asked.

"Number one, stop listening to David's ideas," Nathan said.

"What's your second brilliant idea?" I asked him.

"Let's stop for ice cream!"

And *that* was the best idea I'd heard in a long, long time!

MEET
EDWIN LAND

• • • • • • • • • • • • •

These days, it's pretty easy to get your hands on a nearby cell phone and snap all of the images you want. They instantly appear on the screen, right before your eyes, through the wonder of digital photography.

But long before digital was popular, people had film cameras. They'd put a roll of film in the camera and shoot photos; then they'd have to have that film processed in a laboratory equipped with a darkroom and special chemicals. A few days later, the person who'd taken the photos could pick up prints of the images (plus film negatives—in case they wanted additional copies). There was simply no way of instantly seeing images.

That all changed through the innovation of a scientific researcher who was especially fascinated by the technological possibilities of light. Edwin Land developed many devices that were beneficial to America's military efforts during World War II. But his Polaroid Land Camera (instant photography) stands as perhaps his most significant invention.

It was 1943. "Instant photography" was not even a thought on people's minds. That is, until the day Mr. Land took a photo of his three-year-old daughter—with a film camera—and she asked to see the picture. He said she couldn't; it just wasn't possible. But then, he asked himself . . . why not?

Mr. Land immediately began working with crystals and chemicals to create a camera and a revolutionary type of film that had built-in chemicals . . . so that someone could snap a picture, take a sheet of the film out of the camera, wait sixty seconds, then peel back the negative and see the photo. (It wasn't a *color* photo, and it didn't look as clear as pictures from traditional film cameras, but it was . . . amazing!)

Americans were *thrilled* by this new camera. In fact, the first model of the camera sold out on the very first day it was available.

Over the decades that followed, the Polaroid camera

changed in terms of its shape, size, and picture quality. The Polaroid Company introduced color instant photography in 1963, and later offered film that didn't have a negative attached to it; the picture just popped out of the camera and the image came into view within a few minutes . . . like magic, right before your eyes!

Mr. Land's efforts were recognized with many significant awards, including the National Medal of Technology and the National Medal of Science. He also received the Presidential Medal of Freedom, which is the highest award a civilian (nonmilitary person) can receive in the United States.

Although the appeal of Polaroid products has lessened since digital photography came into our lives, the company still exists, and you can buy one of its cameras if you want instant prints for a party or school gathering.

And to think "instant photography" all began because a three-year-old girl wanted to see her picture right away!

SNAP TO IT!

I can bet that people looked at Mr. Land's development of the Polaroid camera with disbelief. Just think of Mr. Land's friends in his lab:

"Edwin, listen, instant pictures?" one likely said. "That's absurd!"

"You must be sleepwalking. Or sleep-inventing," perhaps someone else told him.

"Yeah"—I'd bet another friend added—"next you'll be telling me that someday there'll be a phone you can carry around in your pocket and play games on and send texts with."

"What are texts?" Mr. Land probably asked.

"I have no idea," I'm sure that friend responded. "I'm just playing the role of a disbeliever in this imaginary play."

"Hey, Eddie, don't take the film out of that oddly shaped camera!" another friend probably told him. "*Wait . . . what are you doing?* You need to handle that in a darkroom! If light hits that film, it'll be ruined. Oh, hey, look, guys—it's a picture of *me*, saying 'Hey, Eddie, don't take the film out of that oddly shaped camera!' *How'd you do that*?"

Some people just don't believe in the possibilties. I hope *you* always believe in the possibilities!

• • • • • • • • • • •

I WOULDN'T DREAM OF IT!

Some people have dreams that are in black and white. Others usually dream in color. And I've never forgotten that my best friend always used to say that before there was photography, people could dream *only* in color.

Why?

Because until photography, there was no way to see the world in black and white. *Everything* was in color!

Makes sense, doesn't it?

My best friend was smart. Maybe that's why he chose me as *his* best friend!

• • • • • • • • • • •

HIS FINGER LINGERED

Back when I was a kid, we had a big, bulky, black-and-white film camera (not a Polaroid). My parents would bring the camera whenever we went on vacation, they'd load it with film, and I'd pose in front of cool buildings and statues, on the beach, at the zoo, and pretty much anywhere and everywhere.

Then we'd get home and my dad would drop off the rolls of film at a camera shop near where he worked. We'd wait a few days, then he'd pick up the envelopes of photos and bring them home so we could all see them together. It was a very exciting way to relive our vacations. Except for the one time I remember when nearly every picture we'd taken in Florida looked like . . .

. . . my dad's finger!

That's right. My dad had taken dozens of photos, and for some reason, his thumb was in front of the lens on almost all of them. It was very disappointing to think I'd see a picture of myself with a live camel, but instead I saw myself with . . . a live finger.

Of course, if we'd had a Polaroid camera (or a digital camera), we would have known to reshoot those photos before our vacation ended.

But that wasn't possible, so today I have fond memories of our trip to Florida, and simply beautiful pictures of my dad's finger.

"SUMMER VACATION 1968"

MEET STEPHANIE KWOLEK

• • • • • • • • • • •

Stephanie Kwolek entered college with a love of fabrics and sewing. After graduating with a degree in chemistry, Ms. Kwolek was interested in attending medical school, but instead joined the DuPont Company as a chemist. Although she saw that as a temporary job in 1946, DuPont is, indeed, where she spent her whole career.

DuPont had long been known for manufacturing fibers, such as nylon and Dacron ®. In 1965, the company was eager to find the next generation of fibers. Recognizing Ms. Kwolek as someone who was eager to experiment, DuPont challenged her to develop a strong and lightweight fiber that could withstand extreme conditions and replace steel in automobile tires.

What Ms. Kwolek came up with was a cloudy solvent that was waterier—and much thinner—than previous chemical compounds. Although this kind of solution was ordinarily discarded, Ms. Kwolek convinced a technician to put it into a spinneret, a device that turns liquid compounds into fibers. (She had to convince him because he was sure the solution would damage the machine.)

It didn't harm the spinneret; instead, it produced something many would call miraculous.

"We spun it, and it spun beautifully," Ms. Kwolek said. "It was very strong and very stiff, unlike anything we had made before."

The result? A fiber sturdier than nylon and 500 percent stronger than steel. In fact, after it was treated with heat, this fiber was nine times stiffer than anything Ms. Kwolek had ever developed. What's more, it was lighter than fiberglass.

Maybe they should have called this fiber Kwolek. Instead, it was given the name Kevlar.

Today, Kevlar is used in so much more than tires; it's a key component of hundreds of applications, including boats, parachutes, skis, helmets, automobile brake linings, aircraft parts, building materials, suspension bridge cables, and even cell phones and frying pans.

Perhaps most important, Kevlar is a bullet-stopping fiber used in protective vests. It's estimated that thousands of law enforcement officials' lives have been saved when they've worn such vests. The same holds true for members of the military.

"I feel very lucky," Ms. Kwolek said. "So many people work all their lives and they don't make a discovery that's of benefit to other people."

Ms. Kwolek's discovery did, indeed, benefit people. Millions of people. And as a result, in 1995, she was enshrined into the National Inventors Hall of Fame (she was the fourth woman so honored, alongside 109 men) in Akron, Ohio. A year later, she was awarded the National Medal of Technology. And she was admitted into the National Women's Hall of Fame in 2003.

Ms. Kwolek had wanted to be an MD, but it's pretty clear she saved more lives as a chemist than she might have as a doctor.

HERE'S MY BRAND-NEW COMIC BOOK!

He's a superhero who's wrapped head-to-toe in Kevlar®!

GET TO KNOW FIBERS AND THEIR USES

Nylon: You'll find this material is often used for lightweight jackets, tents, parachutes, sleeping bags, bathing suits, certain kinds of rope, fishing line, and much more. It is strong and does not tear easily.

Dacron®: A fiber that's useful in the manufacturing of high-pressure fire hoses, curtains, clothing, boat sails, mattresses, and pillows, to name just a few items. It's also strong and resists wrinkles.

Katztron: A fiber that does absolutely nothing, simply because it doesn't exist.

KEVLAR® AND ME

I have a Kevlar house
with Kevlar walls.
My mom wears Kevlar
when duty calls.
I've a Kevlar phone.
And Kevlar skis.
But I can't stand
Kevlar grilled cheese!

INTRODUCING ... KEVLAR® DIAPERS!

So strong, you never have to change them!

If you use regular diapers, you need to change the baby several times a day. But Kevlar Diapers are strong enough to hold it all until that little one is ready for kindergarten . . . and beyond! Use Kevlar Diapers, now available in the convenient 100-pack!

> If a Kevlar Diaper never needs to be changed, why do I need to buy 100?

> In case you have 100 babies!

Kevlar Diapers . . . stronger than you-know-what.

MEET
DR. SALLY RIDE

• • • • • • • • • • •

Y ou learned about astronaut Michael Collins earlier
in this book (unless you skipped those pages,
which you definitely should not have). And while
there have been many other Awesome Achievers who
have gone into space, to me, one stands out as one of
the "Awesomest."

Her name was Sally Ride, and what a ride she took . . .
as the first American woman in space.

In 1978, Dr. Ride earned a doctorate in physics from
Stanford University in California. Just prior to that, while
still in school, she saw an advertisement from NASA in
the Stanford campus newspaper; it said that the space

program was looking for female astronauts. She was one of thousands who applied, and she was selected to participate along with five other women.

A year-long training program followed. After that, Dr. Ride was fully prepared to serve as a mission specialist as part of an upcoming space shuttle crew.

NASA's space shuttle program started in 1981, and it centered around the idea of sending reusable spacecraft into orbit and having them return to Earth to be relaunched for future missions. (In everyday life, a "shuttle" is a train, bus, airplane, or other means of transportation that brings people back and forth on a regular route.)

This concept was revolutionary; previous NASA spacecraft were designed to be used for a single mission.

On June 18, 1983, when STS-7 was launched from Kennedy Space Center in Florida, Dr. Ride was aboard the orbiter known as the *Challenger*. It was the first mission to carry a five-person crew, and Dr. Ride was one of three mission specialist duties. ("STS" stood for Space Shuttle Transportation, and "7" meant it was the seventh mission.)

Among the crew's assignments was the positioning of communications satellites that would remain in orbit, and Dr. Ride's duties included operation of a robotic arm to help set them in place.

The 147-hour mission ended on June 24, 1983, when the *Challenger* returned to Earth and glided to a stop at Edwards Air Force Base in California.

Dr. Ride again went into space on October 5, 1984, aboard STS-41-G. (No, it wasn't the forty-first mission; it was the thirteenth—and the sixth launch of the *Challenger*.) There was a seven-person crew this time, including Dr. Ride and Kathryn Sullivan, who became the first American female to walk in space.

Because *she* didn't get to do that, perhaps Dr. Ride knew how Michael Collins felt!

A few years later, Dr. Ride left the space program and became a teacher, dedicating her life to helping girls and women interested in the study of math and science. So, Dr. Ride is an Awesome Achiever for her work on land as well as in the air.

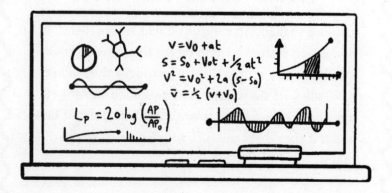

I'M TAKING UP SPACE . . .

In all, Dr. Ride logged 343 hours in space. So here's my question: what on Earth would we have done without her?

Three hundred and forty-three hours in space. Now that's a hero. *My* entire space career also totals 343 hours—that's how long I've spent watching every Star Wars movie over and over and over!

FOOD FOR THOUGHT

According to NASA, meals on the space shuttle were similar to those astronauts might eat at home. I can imagine what Dr. Sally Ride had for breakfast. I can also imagine what Dr. Sally Ride had for dinner.

My only question is . . . what did she have for launch?

LIVING MAPPILY EVER AFTER

I'm sure that the space shuttle had an excellent navigation system to help direct the crew on their interplanetary route. They're just lucky they didn't have the GPS device that's in my car—it *never* gets me where I want to go. Here's what they might have heard if they'd set my GPS for directions to the moon . . .

"Go up.

Continue going up for 234,326 miles.

Slow traffic ahead in 19,234 miles. Please select an alternate route.

Make a U-turn and continue for 3,283 miles.

Toll booth at next exit. Pay $3,000,000.

Continue up for 27,093 miles.

You have arrived at your destination. Welcome to Jupiter."

Caution . . . meteor shower ahead!

MEET DR. ROY J. PLUNKETT

• • • • • • • • • • •

Polytetrafluoroethylene. It's extremely hard to pronounce. In fact, it took me less time to write this book than it did to learn how to say that word.

Why did I *want to* say that word? Because, quite simply, it's the (unplanned) discovery of Dr. Roy J. Plunkett, and it's very likely that you have some polytetrafluoroethylene in your home.

What *is* polytetrafluoroethylene? It's the slipperiest material on Earth, and the main reason foods don't stick in the kitchen pots and pans. Oh, and I should probably tell you that the more common name for polytetrafluoroethylene is Teflon™. Perhaps you've heard *that* word.

Here's the whole (nonsticky) story. . . .

Like Ms. Kwolek, Dr. Plunkett was a chemist at the DuPont Company. He was working with gases in the lab, trying to perfect one for use as a refrigerant (which would keep things cool). To his surprise, he discovered that one particular gas he had frozen had changed its chemical form, thereby leaving him with a cylinder full of a white, waxy material (polytetrafluoroethylene). He was disappointed . . . until he found that polytetrafluoroethylene (or PTFE; I'm so glad we don't have to keep saying that whole long word!) was resistant to heat and had very low surface friction, so other substances wouldn't stick to it.

What a discovery!

Before long, cookware that had been sprayed with a PTFE (or Teflon™) coating was offered for sale. Instead of having to scrape food out of the pots and pans after it had been heated, people watched with amazement as it just slid right out.

But the appeal of PTFE extends far beyond the kitchen. It has also been used on fabrics to help keep them stain-free. Plus, because it's so smooth and slippery, can withstand high heat, and doesn't crack easily, PTFE has proven to be an important substance in virtually every major industry—including electronics, construction, automobiles (windshield wipers that glide back and forth), and even cosmetics (it's what helps nail polish stay strong!).

Dr. Plunkett spent nearly forty years at DuPont, and he was welcomed into both the Plastics Hall of Fame and the National Inventors Hall of Fame. Just how did the scientist feel about his "accidental" discovery? He simply said that he was pleased to have come up with an invention that "has been of great personal benefit to people—not just indirectly, but directly to real people whom I know."

If only he'd taken the time to invent an original name shorter than polytetrafluoroethylene!

PLEASE NOTE: THE BOTTOM OF THIS PAGE HAS BEEN SPRAYED WITH PTFE

Unfortunately, the words I wanted to share below have slid off of the

paper.

So r r y !

Why wouldn't I have made a good scientist? Because instead of calling it polytetrafluoroethylene, I'd have called it poly-blah-blah-blah-blah-blah!

WARNING! WARNING! WARNING! (DON'T SAY I DIDN'T WARN YOU!)

As I said, PTFE is often used in fabrics, and it's the slipperiest material on Earth. Here's some ways to tell if they've put *too much* PTFE in your articles of clothing:

You slide down the playground slide and you land in Cleveland (unless you're *starting* in Cleveland—then it's okay).

You sit down at the dining room table and you end up *under* the dining room table.

You find you can glide across the ice rink without skates on.

You put your hat on your head at school, and it flies off and lands on your brother's head (and *he's* at home!).

You put on a pair of earmuffs and they end up covering the back of your head . . . and your nose.

AND NOW ... PRESENTING A VERY IMPORTANT RIDDLE BASED ON THE WONDERFUL DISCOVERY OF DR. ROY J. PLUNKETT:

Q: Dr. Plunkett's dog loved to play fetch. What did the pup invent?
A: The nonstick stick!

Get it? You don't? (Neither did the dog, because the stick wouldn't . . . stick!)

MEET
DR. SPENCER SILVER
AND ARTHUR FRY

S peaking of sticky...

... chances are your life is full of those little scraps of paper that people call "sticky notes." But do you know who invented them (clearly *not* Dr. Roy J. Plunkett— his invention *stopped* things from sticking)?

Rather, the notes were an idea that came from Dr. Spencer Silver and Arthur Fry, although they didn't exactly work *together* on the project.

Back in 1968, Dr. Silver was a senior chemist developing adhesive (glue) technology in a research lab at the 3M Company. Now, usually when you glue things together, those items *stay* together. But during his

research, Dr. Silver came up with a reusable glue
that allowed items to be peeled apart even after they'd
been attached.

For many years, Dr. Silver couldn't find anyone in the
company who was interested in his unique, only-slightly
sticky glue. But Dr. Silver "stuck to it!" (Get it? Stuck to it.
That's a joke, dear reader!)

"I got to be known as 'Mr. Persistent,'" Dr. Silver once
said (although he probably should have called himself *Dr.*
Persistent). "Because I wouldn't give up."

And he didn't have to give up. Because one day, Dr.
Silver eventually met Arthur Fry, another 3M scientist, at
a company meeting.

Amazingly, Mr. Fry had a problem that called for
an only-slightly sticky glue. See, Mr. Fry sang with his
church choir, and he kept losing his place in his book of
hymns because the paper he used as page markings kept
falling out.

He needed bookmarks that would stay in place yet not
do damage to his book.

He needed Dr. Silver's glue!

The two men worked together to create small notes
with the new glue on them—which perfectly solved
Mr. Fry's problem. 3M first released them as Press 'n
Peel pads. "I thought, what we have here isn't just a

bookmark," said Mr. Fry about the joint effort. "It's a whole new way to communicate."

After a while, they changed the name to Post-it® Notes, and it became a huge success. "This is a product that looks so simple but is very high-tech," Mr. Fry once said.

More than 50 billion Post-it® Notes are sold every year, and there are more than 4,000 Post-it® products available worldwide. Dr. Silver's glue technology is also part of medical bandages and decorating kits among countless other uses.

Not bad for an invention that only came together because of one man's belief in his idea . . . and another man's need!

STICKY THINKING

The license plate on Mr. Fry's car reads POSTIT. (That's true!)

Dr. Plunkett ordered a license plate that read POLYTETRAFLUOROETHYLENE, but it made the car too wide to fit on the highway! (That's *not* true!)

EVEN STICKIER THINKING

It took twelve years from the time Dr. Silver invented his glue until Post-it® Notes were offered for sale.

Can you imagine—twelve years!

I have an idea for a new product that will be the best thing anyone has ever seen, ever used, or ever tasted. It will truly change the world.

What is it?

Ask me in thirteen years.

AND THE STICKIEST THINKING OF ALL...

Dr. Silver obviously enjoyed great success from his role in the introduction of Post-it® Notes. But he once said his real satisfaction comes from seeing them in movies and also from knowing that they're being used by millions of people every day. To quote Dr. Silver, "The fact that the Post-It Notes just exploded as a product is more than I could ever hope for."

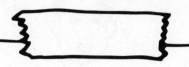

Dear Dr. Silver,

I am very, very impressed by your discovery of a glue that doesn't actually glue things together. I think of myself as an inventor, too, and I'd love to know what you think about some of my recent inventions.

How about . . .

Bubble gum that you can't actually use to blow bubbles?

Shampoo that doesn't actually clean your hair?

A bathing suit that you can't wear in the water (it's not waterproof)?

A stapler that doesn't hold any staples?

A watch that doesn't tell you the time?

Scissors that don't cut anything.

Or . . .

. . . are you ready for this?

Dog food that dogs won't eat.

I am very excited by all of these ideas, and if you like them, too, please show this list to Mr. Fry; perhaps he's got another problem that one of *my* discoveries can solve.

MEET
DR. HUGH HERR

. . . .

It's sad but true that there are approximately two million people in America who have had one or more limbs amputated (removed) due to injury or for medical reasons. These men, women, and children face challenges to be sure, but with courage and determination, they are able to lead full and productive lives.

Dr. Hugh Herr, an engineer and biochemist, is making significant contributions to the movement and well-being of those who've lost limbs. As the head of the Biomechatronics Group within the MIT (Massachusetts Institute of Technology) Media Lab, he leads a team that designs bionic—superhuman, robotic—limbs that aim to deliver much of the feeling and function that human arms and legs do.

Perhaps this is a good time to tell you that Dr. Herr isn't simply a gifted scientist. He is also someone who has had his limbs amputated—he lost both of his legs below the knees after suffering frostbite following a mountain climbing accident.

Dr. Herr was told he would never be able to go climbing again. But after designing his own prosthetic (artificial) limbs out of rubber, metal, and wood, he developed the world's first bionic lower leg, called the BiOM Ankle System (it has three built-in computers, each the size of a fingernail, that control motors to help the user stand, walk, or even run).

What's more, Dr. Herr now holds more than forty patents related to his work in the field of "wearable robotics." They include the computer-controlled knee, which automatically adjusts to the individual who's wearing it, which gives a disabled person the chance to regain mobility—and even participate in many physical activities—perhaps in a way they never thought could be possible.

Did Dr. Herr ever return to mountain climbing? You'd better believe he did. In fact, he does much more than that. As he once said, "When you go into my closet, there are many, many pairs of legs. I have a running pair, I have a bionic walking pair, limbs that are waterproof . . . I have various legs to climb mountains and to sense steep ice walls."

To be sure, Dr. Herr's inspiring personal story is one of triumph. But it seems to me that his professional story—and the work that he and his team are doing to make life better for so many others—just may be even more triumphant.

WHAT'S THE GOOD WORD? BEATS ME!

I greatly admire Dr. Herr, both for his brilliant scientific mind and for the generosity of spirit he showed in sharing his inventions with the world.

If I ever met this Awesome Achiever, I might not know what to say. My words might get scrambled and I'd be totally tongue-tied. The conversation would probably go something like this:

DR. HERR: Hello, I'm Hugh.

ALAN: No, you're not. *I'm* me.

DR. HERR: I mean, I'm Hugh.

ALAN: No, I said *I'm* me. As for you . . .

DR. HERR: Yes?

ALAN: Yes, what?

DR. HERR: I heard my name.

ALAN: You did?

DR. HERR: Yes, you said Hugh.

ALAN: I did?

DR. HERR: Yes, *you* did.

ALAN: Should we start over?

DR. HERR: No, I'm a very busy man. I'm through with you. And that means *you're* through with Hugh, too.

ALAN: In that case . . .

DR. HERR: Yes?

ALAN: Toodle-oo to you, Hugh!

3-D, OR NOT 3-D? ... THAT IS THE QUESTION

If you ask me, Dr. Herr is an Awesome Achiever ... and a true genius. It's fascinating to think that human body parts can now be replaced with functioning, machine-made elements. The process, called bioprinting, is constantly being improved, so scientists can use 3-D printers—in conjunction with human cells—to literally "print" heart valves, organs, tissue, and other essential parts.

So, the famous line from Shakespeare's *Julius Caesar* will soon have to be rewritten, from "Friends, Romans, countrymen, lend me your ears," to "Friends, Romans, countrymen, *print* me an ear."

Can I have a hand for that joke? No? Never mind ... I'll print one myself!

THE MATTER IS CLOTHED

I've never been mountain climbing. I've never been rock climbing. I have, however, shown true courage and bravery and climbed to the very top of . . . Mount Clothes.

Where's Mount Clothes? In my son Nathan's room. It's a pile of dirty socks, shirts, pants, sweats, and more. It's absolutely breathtaking—and I don't mean the height. It's the *smell*. The kid simply won't do laundry.

And never mind *washing* his clothes. What's worse (and this is 100 percent true), for a long time, Nathan refused to *buy* new underwear. He had two favorite pairs of boxer shorts, and he'd alternate, wearing each one every other day.

I once said to him, "That's disgusting. Don't they stink?" And he replied, "Nah. I keep the one I'm not wearing on my bedroom fan. The breeze from the fan airs them out overnight."

In an important related story, my oldest son used to be laundry-challenged as well. I remember when he first went away to college, he called and complained to me: "I put my dirty clothing in the machine, added soap, and turned it on. When it stopped, the clothes came out hot and soapy."

I told him, "You obviously put them in the dryer."

He said, "It can't be the dryer. It's the machine on the left side."

I informed him that our dryer at home was on the left side, and the washing machine was on the right. But that was only how *we* set them up. There's no strict rule.

So, let's review. What have we learned?

1. Wash your garments often to avoid your own Mount Clothes.

2. Don't keep your underwear on the fan overnight.

3. Don't put dirty laundry and soap in the dryer. Unless, of course, you enjoy hot, soapy clothes.

Thank you.

A FINAL WORD
FROM ALAN KATZ

~~~~~~~~

Chimpanzee.

What? That's my final word.

Sorry, that it has nothing whatsoever to do with this book.

I hope you had a good time reading about these Awesome Achievers in science. I hope that you've learned a lot and had a ton of fun. And I hope that you'll take the time to find out even more about the incredible people you just read about.

Most of all, I hope you'll share this book with friends. If you liked it, chances are they will too.

Make sense? I sure hope so. And, hey, if you have ideas for future Awesome Achievers books, please write to me at awesomeachievers@gmail.com.

Thanks. I gotta go now. . . . They need me at the Museum of Underwear (but, like Kevlar Man, I won't touch anything!).

Bye!

NOTES